P9-CAL-697

THANKSGIVING

More Than 50 Years of Celebrating Life's Most Treasured Moments

Vol. 59, No. 5

Earth with her thousand voices praises God.
—Samuel Taylor Coleridge

IDEALS—Vol. 59, No. 5 September MMII IDEALS (ISSN 0019-137X, USPS 256-240) is published six times a year: January, March, May, July, September, and November by IDEALS PUBLICATIONS, a division of Guideposts 39 Seminary Hill Road, Carmel, NY 10512.

Printed on Weyerhaeuser Husky. The paper used in this publication meets the minimum requirements of American National Standard for Information Sciences— Permanence of Paper for Printed Library Materials, ANSI Z39.48-1984.

Periodicals postage paid at Carmel, New York, and additional mailing offices. POSTMASTER: Send address changes to Ideals, 39 Seminary Hill Road, Carmel, NY 10512. For subscription or customer service questions, contact Ideals Publications, a division of Guideposts, 39 Seminary Hill Road, Carmel, NY 10512. Fax 845-228-2115.

ISBN 0-8249-1203-9 GST 893989236

Visit the *Ideals* website at www.idealsbooks.com

Cover Photo: The Washington Park Arboretum in Seattle, Washington. Photo by Terry Donnelly.
Inside Front Cover: LEAVES A'BLOOM. *Mary Kay Krell, artist.*
Inside Back Cover: A TUMBLE OF LEAVES, CORNWALL. *Charles Summers, artist.*
Image from Chisholm Gallery, West Palm Beach, Florida/Superstock.

GIVE *ideals* THIS CHRISTMAS . . . Let *ideals* express your heartfelt wishes at every season of the year!

WE'LL SEND A GIFT ANNOUNCEMENT WITH THE FIRST ISSUE!

Every issue of *Ideals* is bursting with a celebration of life's special times: Christmas, Thanksgiving, Easter, Mother's Day, Country and Friendship. Give a gift subscription to *Ideals* this Christmas and you will bring joy to the lives of special people six times a year! Each issue offers page after page of magnificent photographs, exquisite drawings and paintings, delightful stories and poetry.

Each is a "keeper" that invites the reader back, again and again, to look, read and ponder. There's nothing quite as special as a gift of *Ideals*!

SAVE 44%
off the bookstore price!
To order, mail card below

Preferred Subscriber Guarantee

1. We guarantee that you may cancel your subscription(s) at any time upon request and that you will receive a prompt refund on any unserved issues.

2. We guarantee to continue your gift subscription(s) at the then current rate for as long as you wish, without interruption, unless you instruct us to stop.

3. We guarantee if you extend your own subscription we will also provide continuous service at the then current rate for as long as you wish.

4. Send no money now. As a Preferred Subscriber, a gift card will be automatically sent in your name every year (on receipt of payment) to the person named.

---

ideals CHRISTMAS GIFT LIST — PREFERRED SUBSCRIBER

❑ YES! Please send a one-year *Ideals* gift subscription to my friends listed below.

❑ $19.95 enclosed for each ❑ Bill me $19.95 for each

MY NAME:

_____
NAME

_____
ADDRESS

_____
CITY   STATE   ZIP
❑ Please also enter a subscription for myself

SEND A GIFT SUBSCRIPTION TO:

_____
NAME

_____
ADDRESS

_____
CITY   STATE   ZIP

SEND A GIFT SUBSCRIPTION TO:

_____
NAME

_____
ADDRESS

_____
CITY   STATE   ZIP

For addresses outside the U.S.A., annual rate is $29.95 payable in U.S. funds.

EKT0AA

05-201975950

---

ideals CHRISTMAS GIFT LIST — PREFERRED SUBSCRIBER

❑ YES! Please send a one-year *Ideals* gift subscription to my friends listed below.

❑ $19.95 enclosed for each ❑ Bill me $19.95 for each

MY NAME:

_____
NAME

_____
ADDRESS

_____
CITY   STATE   ZIP
❑ Please also enter a subscription for myself

SEND A GIFT SUBSCRIPTION TO:

_____
NAME

_____
ADDRESS

_____
CITY   STATE   ZIP

SEND A GIFT SUBSCRIPTION TO:

_____
NAME

_____
ADDRESS

_____
CITY   STATE   ZIP

For addresses outside the U.S.A., annual rate is $29.95 payable in U.S. funds.

EKT0AA

05-201975950

Do your Christmas shopping today and
SAVE 44%

off the regular bookstore price of *Ideals* when you give a one-year subscription!

ONLY
$19⁹⁵

Everyone knows at least two or three people who would love a gift subscription to *Ideals*! It's a very special Christmas gift that keeps on reminding a close friend or relative of your thoughtfulness all through the year. And, when you order now, you enjoy a generous savings off the regular bookstore price—and do your Christmas shopping right away!

for each one-year gift subscription of six issues— a savings of $15.75 off the bookstore price.

To order today, use one or both of the postage-paid reply cards (see reverse side).

Add more gifts, if you wish, by enclosing a separate list with the additional names and addresses and mail in an envelope to:

Ideals Publications, Inc.
A Division of Guideposts
P.O. Box 1410
Carmel, NY 10512-7910

SEND NO MONEY NOW—WE'LL BILL YOU LATER!

Orders received after December 1 will start with the Easter issue.

Autumn Stroll

Barbara A. Poindexter

A rabbit scampers neath a log;
A dying tree now sways and creaks
As gentle breezes waft the fog
And place sweet coolness on my cheeks.

The leaves crunch softly neath my feet;
The mist lays droplets on my hair.
The autumn time indeed is sweet
As rich, full odors fill the air.

The leaves of color round me fall
In coolness of the autumn's shade.
I walk on slowly, seeing all
This glorious season God has made.

Walking Tours

Robert Louis Stevenson

Now, to be properly enjoyed, a walking tour should be gone upon alone. . . . And then you must be open to all impressions and let your thoughts take color from what you see. You should be as a pipe for any wind to play upon. . . . There should be no cackle of voices at your elbow to jar on the meditative silence of the morning. And so long as a man is reasoning, he cannot surrender himself to that fine intoxication that comes of much motion in the open air, that begins in a sort of dazzle and sluggishness of the brain and ends in a peace that passes comprehension.

A covered footbridge offers a shady spot to watch the creek in Willard Brook State Park, Massachusetts. Photo by William H. Johnson.

October

Josephine Powell Beaty

Summer lingers though the woods
Are filled with winter's prophecy
In thinning leaves and russet tones
Of red and yellow tracery.

The morning boasts the songs of birds,
And night is routed gallantly.
But twilight hears the cricket's call
With rhythmic, shrill insistency.

Now from the woods new voices come:
The owl complaining to the moon,
And, echoing through the leafy vault,
The eerie laughter of the loon.

Thin frost upon the meadowland,
A trail of birds across the sky—
A keenness fills the vibrant air
That sends the dead leaves whirling by.

*This page: Leaves pepper a picnic area in West Virginia's
Blackwater Falls State Park. Photo by Carr Clifton.
Overleaf: A lake in East Washington, New Hampshire, provides a spectacular
mirror image of an autumn treeline. Photo by William H. Johnson.*

Autumn Gold

Roberta Carpenter

Pumpkins, brushed orange by the summer sun,
Lie helter-skelter along the trail of twisted green
Vines that wind snake-like across the field from
Fence to fence and creek to woods. As soft as
Angel wings, an early morning frost covers fruit
And vine in a blanket of gray shadows then drifts
Into nothingness as a playful breeze teases green
Leaves edged in chocolate and curled with age.

The old man walks silently between his sea green
Plots and, with hat pulled low against the blush
Of the rising sun, beholds the necklace of burnished
Round balls that trace designs of fall fantasy across
The landscape. A birdcall echoes in a cloudless sky,
And autumn leaves dance and spin in an
Arrogant display to fall like a crazy quilt
Upon the old man's autumn gold.

Pumpkins are brushed by the sun in Springfield, Oregon.
Photo by Dennis Frates.

Country CHRONICLE

Lansing Christman

UNTO THE HILLS

I have had hills around me all my life. They have been in different parts of the country, but they are the result of the same creative forces of nature. For my first sixty years, I was a part of the Helderhills in upstate New York. I was born in them, played in them, and, like my father and grandfather before me, I worked in them. These were the hills from which my father wrote his songs of poetry. For more than thirty years now, I have been in the foothills of the Blue Ridge in northern South Carolina. In these hills too I have worked and I have walked. And like my father, I have harvested my songs in poetry and prose.

In both parts of the country, I have watched the seasons march across the hills: the sere brown fields of November, the winter snow, the flowers of spring, the serenity of summer. Birds and blossoms and trees know the same march of time.

The hills raise themselves up to be touched by both the subtleties and the extremes of the sweep of the year. Rich hours of sun, stars, clouds, rain, and snow all keep coming in their turn. The moisture of a rain is nourishing to earth and root. A winter snow is cleansing and soothing. A spring sun brings leafing and blooming, and that of summer brings ripening. And they all offer me much of which to think and to write as I walk.

And here at Thanksgiving, "I will lift up mine eyes unto the hills." How articulate these hills are in what they say to me in poetry and prose! How sweet and rich and endearing!

The author of three books, Lansing Christman has contributed to Ideals *for almost thirty years. Mr. Christman has also been published in several American, international, and braille anthologies. He lives in rural South Carolina.*

Hills in Peacham, Vermont, form a patchwork of color. Photo by William H. Johnson.

A sycamore towers over a field in Missouri. Photo by Gay Bumgarner.

A TREE TO GROW WITH
Barbara Fousek

An enormous sycamore reigns over our backyard. From the broad girth of its trunk, great silver branches spread heavenward, at once uplifting and sheltering. In its lofty presence, our family has found joy and comfort for all our years here.

We first entered the magic realm of this benevolent monarch on a sunny August afternoon twenty years ago. Transferred suddenly from the East to Saint Louis, my husband made a hurried preliminary trip and contracted for a suburban house he had seen only briefly.

And now it was moving day. Driving down the long, sloping street to our new home, I took in the trim greenness of the subdivision's hedges and the splash of pink petunias snug in their brick planters. And I mourned, thinking of our three young children and how much they enjoyed the openness and freedom of the rolling countryside we had left behind.

Then, drawing nearer, I saw the huge sycamore towering above the low-slung roof of our ranch-style house and waving a gentle welcome with its branches. Our children saw it too. Scarcely had our luggage-laden station wagon come to a halt in the driveway than they tumbled out, their first eager steps drawn irresistibly to the backyard. My husband and I joined them. All of us stared in awe.

"Some tree," my husband said. "I really hadn't noticed it before. Must have been around for two hundred years."

Our five-year-old son, eyes widening, mouth agape, followed the pale trunk skyward and whispered only a reverent "Wow." Silently I thanked whomever, by plan or whim, had spared this generous giant. I knew somehow that all would be well with us here; that this too could be a place for growing. And so it has been.

On our first morning, exuberant shouts startled us all from sleep. The children scurried outside to find no one. Then from the thick green foliage above their heads came laughter and the outstretched arms of newfound friends. From that moment their world expanded in a new direction—up! Open fields were forgotten in the joys of a playground in the sky.

A would-be astronaut soared spaceward in his rocket swing. With piercing call, Tarzan on his rope vine cut a graceful arc high above the jungle floor. A pirate, aloft in the crow's nest of his prowling galleon, searched the horizon for prey. In more pensive mood, one could simply hide away in those sheltering arms—to read, to dream, to gaze into blue infinity.

Drawing nearer, I saw the huge sycamore towering above the low-slung roof of our ranch-style house and waving a gentle welcome with its branches.

The great tree also understood more earthbound needs and pleasures. That sturdy trunk knew the tug of the volleyball net, a thousand slaps of small hands touching base for hide-and-seek. Broad leaves sheltered backyard picnickers, the lounging bookworm, and the sandbox set patting out mudpies. Laced with twinkling lights, the leafy branches roofed many a teenage party in starry, emerald splendor.

But time has passed, and things are quieter now. A frayed bit of rope flutters from a lofty branch. Tarzan's shrill cry has given way to the trill of birds and the muffled purr of distant highway traffic. How often my heart returns to those livelier scenes.

Today is such a day. I wander about the yard, noting the changes, wondering—does the tree miss those clambering bodies and the joyous shouts? Then, fingering the bark, I discover something that had escaped me. Long ago, for the youngest sky-bound children, my husband had lodged a small ladder against the sycamore's trunk. Now it is firmly embedded. Slowly, with unceasing rhythm, the tree gnarled its way around the top of the metal posts, fashioning a permanent stairway to the sky. My foot lifts instinctively to the first rung. Resting it there, I ponder, my vision lifted upward by that silvery column as a little boy's was long ago. One more rung—then suddenly past, present, and future blend. Of course! There will be more eager young feet climbing here. Perhaps even those of my grandchildren. I see swinging arms and legs, and again rippling laughter falls on the soft autumn air.

Leaning against the little ladder, I share its oneness with the towering sycamore. As I lift my eyes to the soaring branches that sway serenely above me, I feel anew the enduring wonder of growth; and I am at peace—with myself and with change, even as the tree.

Thoughts on an Autumn Evening

Katherine Edelman

Birds in number congregate,
Chattering in long debate.
With the thinning of the bough
They discuss their leaving now.

Watching them, I know that soon
They will soar where sun and moon
Glow above a warmer land
Than the one on which I stand.

Birdfeeder

Rebecca Sellers Terrible

Little birds feed on thistle seed,
The chickadees, finches, and wrens.
The doves all go to the snow below
And catch what falls to them.

The squirrels, those clowns, hang upside down
To see what they can steal.
And here I peek from the window seat
And watch the merry meal.

Autumn Visitors

Emily Romano

Among red leaves now edged with gold,
The buntings perch and flit and scold;
Each slender line of throat and breast
So delicate, yet filled with zest,
As two by two they gaily mince
Upon the branches of the quince.

A nest is tucked among the autumn leaves in Sierra Nevada, California.
Photo by Londie G. Padelsky.

From My Garden Journal

Lisa Ragan

QUINCE

Americans traditionally celebrate Thanksgiving with the kind of gusto that employs all five senses; but for me, Thanksgiving has always been foremost about aroma. My memories of past Thanksgivings are all inextricably intertwined with particular scents of the season—decaying leaves scattered on the lawn, burning logs in the fireplace, and my grandmother's apple tree heavy with fragrant fruit. And then there's all those wonderful kitchen smells! Roast turkey, pumpkin pie, and mulled cider all put me in mind of family get-togethers with plenty of leftovers.

I've often wondered what aromas the early Colonists might have enjoyed while they celebrated the first Thanksgiving so many ages ago. Historians disagree about the different foods that may or may not have been enjoyed at that original harvest meal, but records state that early settlers of the New World brought with them the treasured quince fruit; at first they even planted more

quince trees than apple or pear trees. Although I have no proof that the quince played a featured part at the first Thanksgiving, I do know that it remained a favorite of the Colonists for many years and that it makes excellent pies and preserves. And as for fragrance, the quince possesses a distinctive, unusual aroma that proves heavenly for some and too intense for others. The scent is so strong, in fact, that a single quince fruit lying in a bowl on the kitchen table can perfume an entire home.

A native to the Middle East, quince became a symbol of fertility for the ancient Greeks and Romans, who equated the quince with love and happiness and even dedicated this remarkable fruit to Venus, the Roman goddess of love. In later centuries, the Emperor Charlemagne included quince trees, pruned into neat hedges, in his royal gardens. By the year 1570, even the Pope recognized the exquisite characteristics of the quince: historical documents describe a grand banquet given by Pope Pius V that included a quince in every pastry.

The quince traveled to the New World with the early Colonists; and at its height of popularity here, every dooryard kitchen garden included at least one quince tree. But soon the quince proved a bit too fragile for the cold winters in the northern colonies and was replaced by its hardier cousins, apple and pear. Today, gardeners are rediscovering this fruit of our yesteryear and experimenting with delectable dishes such as quince pie, quince jelly, and quince honey.

With their relatively small stature (reaching heights of only ten to fifteen feet) and their

QUINCE

unusual, twisted branches, quince trees add a striking element to the landscape. Early spring prompts the quince tree to bloom large, single flowers of soft pink or snowy white on each of the branch tips. Foliage ranges in color from light green to gray-green. By late October or November, large globes of yellow-orange fruit will be nearly ripe. The quince tree produces fruit that is hard and sometimes bumpy; about five inches in diameter; covered in light fuzz; and round, oblong, or pear-shaped. Quince fruit ranges in color from green to yellow to honey-amber.

The fruit's strong aroma can penetrate neighboring fruits or vegetables if stored together. Some cooks purposely blend sliced apples with sliced quince to add an interesting flavor and fragrance to the apples. They usually remove the quince slices before serving, since quince is seldom eaten raw; it proves too sour and tough for most palates. But the fruit transforms into a luscious and tender substance of pink hue when sweetened and stewed or baked. Many quince fans argue that one can substitute quince for apples in any baked apple dish, including pie and cobbler. The quince also has a naturally high pectin content, which makes it ideal for jellies and preserves. Some cooks use quince fruit to flavor apple butter or honey for an interesting alternative.

A number of quince varieties have been developed over the years, including the pineapple variety, which produces fruit that can be eaten raw. The orange variety dates back to the nineteenth century and yields a fruit with deep, rich-colored flesh and strong flavor. Another heirloom variety is Smyrna, which made its way to America in 1897 from Turkey. Other varieties include Champion (a slight lemon flavor), Jumbo, Golden, Meech, Portugal, and Van Deman (a somewhat spicy flavor).

Even though quince trees are not as hardy as their apple and pear relatives, they usually grow well where pear trees thrive. Quince trees cannot tolerate winters that reach temperatures colder than –15° F. Experts recommend planting quince in a sunny location with well-drained soil and no closer than fifteen feet to any neighboring tree. When selecting a quince specimen, take care to select a tree of the genus *Cydonia oblonga*. Gardeners sometime confuse it with flowering quince, *Chaenomeles japonica*, which is also called Japanese quince and is a different plant altogether. The flowering quince grows into an ornamental shrub that produces small green fruits of inferior quality but that can also be used in preserves.

Quince trees grow slowly and require little fertilizer and little pruning once established. They do self-pollinate, an unusual trait among fruit trees. This means that gardeners need only plant a single quince tree to enjoy a bounty of this unique fruit within one to two years. When harvesting, the fruit should break from the tree without undue force and should be picked with care because it tends to bruise easily.

Concerning diseases, quince trees can be susceptible to fire blight, which is a bacterial disease. Applying too much fertilizer can increase the quince tree's vulnerability to fire blight. Two fungal diseases that can afflict the quince include cedar-quince rust or cedar-hawthorn rust, and two pests that can harm the quince include the codling moth and the oriental fruit moth. Experts recommend selecting disease-resistant varieties of trees; ask local nursery personnel for the best varieties for your area.

Although I have not yet planted a quince tree in my own garden, I do intend to seek out some of its curious fruit for this year's Thanksgiving dinner. My family will no doubt be surprised when I arrive at Grandmother's house with a quince pie or quince-apple butter; but by serving a dish from Colonial times, we honor America's history on the day we give thanks to God for harvest and health.

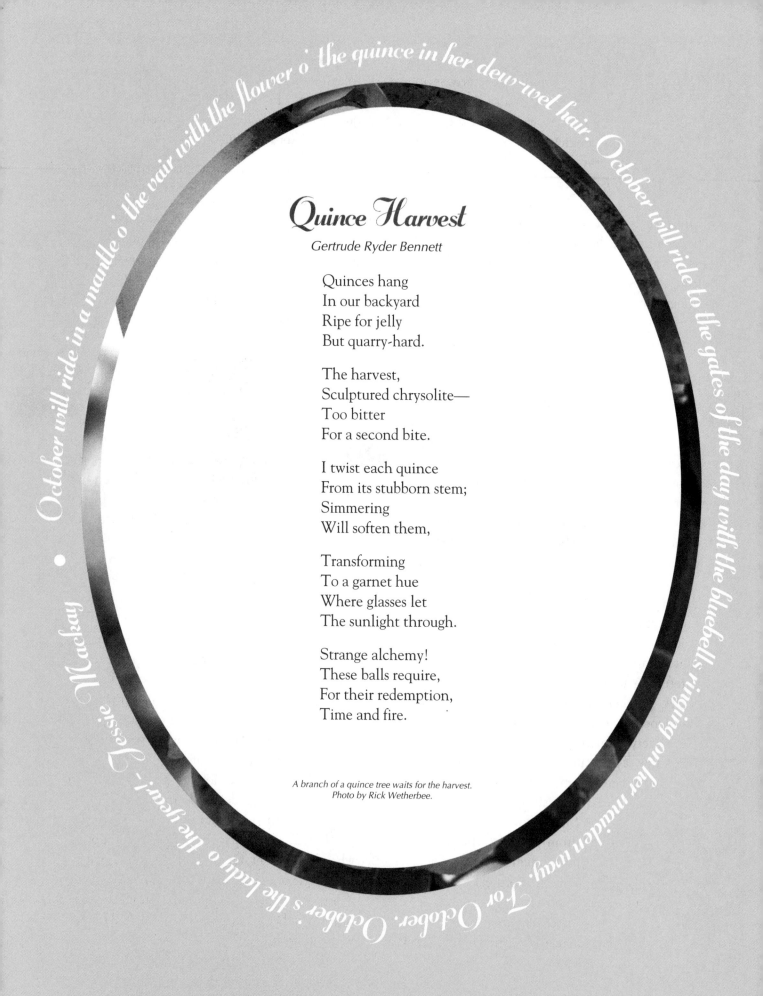

Quince Harvest

Gertrude Ryder Bennett

Quinces hang
In our backyard
Ripe for jelly
But quarry-hard.

The harvest,
Sculptured chrysolite—
Too bitter
For a second bite.

I twist each quince
From its stubborn stem;
Simmering
Will soften them,

Transforming
To a garnet hue
Where glasses let
The sunlight through.

Strange alchemy!
These balls require,
For their redemption,
Time and fire.

A branch of a quince tree waits for the harvest.
Photo by Rick Wetherbee.

October will ride in a mantle o' the vair with the flower o' the quince in her dew-wet hair. October will ride to the gates of the day with the bluebells ringing on her maiden way. For October, October's the lady o' the year! — Jessie Mackay

Autumn Winds

Alice M. Swaim

Autumn winds turn grape leaves silver,
Set the poplars whispering,
Light the flames on sumac torches,
Teach the withered sedge to sing.

Autumn winds send wild geese soaring,
Dark against the harvest moon,
Drive us in for warmth and shelter,
Hint of snowflakes flying soon.

Autumn Wind

Arthur Thatcher

The autumn wind is searching for a place
Where it may pile the season's falling leaves;
It visits hollows in the woodland grove
And grasps at bushes that it bends and weaves.

The autumn wind takes little time for rest
As nature now prepares for winter days.
The breeze must spread protective coverlets
Where life may hide on frozen windswept ways.

October flowers, departing butterflies,
And full-blown blossoms of the goldenrod
Are all caressed by autumn's restless wind
As handiworks of earth and nature's God.

Autumn Afternoon

Grace V. Watkins

I heard a little vagabonding
Wind tiptoe along
A warm, sunlighted autumn hill
And sing a golden song.
I watched a flame-bright oriole
And heard the sweet salute
Of shimmering notes he played upon
His tiny crystal flute.
Then suddenly within my heart
A joy-wide glory shone,
And all the lovely, lifting dreams
That I had ever known.

A windmill waits for the next autumn breeze in THE WINDMILL
by Karl Cartier. Image from Superstock.

Readers' Reflections

Editor's Note: Readers are invited to submit original poetry for possible publication in future issues of Ideals. Please send typed copies only; manuscripts will not be returned. Writers receive $10 for each published submission. Send material to Readers' Reflections, Ideals Publications, 535 Metroplex Drive, Suite 250, Nashville, Tennessee 37211.

Autumn Decorations

Joanne M. Babay
Erie, Pennsylvania

Shall I tell about the bittersweet,
A trailing vine wild woodlands share?
It wraps around her branch and limb,
Ensnarls within her maiden hair.
You cannot penetrate its growth
With simple flower and twisting stem.
It multiplies along fencerows
Till harvest's frost reveals its gem.
A golden shell protects its bead,
The seed inside, a berry red.
Pod cracked, then reaped
    from woodland niche,
To grace home, hearth,
    and wreath instead.

Things to Give Thanks For

Vickie Petrey
Brodhead, Kentucky

Golden leaves on autumn trees,
The salty spray of an ocean breeze,
The sun that rises at the dawn,
The vibrant green of a summer lawn,
The laughter of a little child,
Flowers blooming thick and wild,
Corn and wheat and new potatoes,
Beans and squash and red tomatoes,
Rain to make the good things grow,
Lacy flakes of falling snow,
The smile of a dear old friend,
Broken hearts that finally mend,
Seeds into the rich earth planted,
And a million things we take for granted.

The Beauty of Autumn

Catherine Donalson
Fort Myers, Florida

When Autumn takes
   her brush in hand
And paints in colors bold,
Then every tree
   throughout the land
Is dressed in red and gold.
The sturdy oak,
   the dogwood tree
Decked out in full array
Defy the brilliance
   of the sun,
Their foliage to display.
Triumphantly all nature sings
And all mankind is blest
That God conceived
   a masterpiece,
His love to manifest.

The Dance of Autumn

Roberta Carpenter
Goshen, Indiana

In colorful disarray they fall from twig and bough,
Brazenly splashed, radiantly colored, arrogantly displayed
In vivid hues of orange and red and yellow,
Sprinkled with playful streaks of summer green that
Spill undisciplined across frost-nipped leaf and stem.

Undaunted, unafraid, spinning, spiraling,
A macabre dance, buoyant in free-falling splendor,
A parade of autumn leaves whirling in dizzying descent
To plunge, a crazy quilt of many colors,
A silent onslaught upon the barren ground.

Heavenward

Dorothy B. Taggart

For those who sense the time the wild geese fly,
There is a sorrow on an autumn day.
They hear the leaving song across the sky—
A fugue, crescendoing from far away.

And high above the morning's silver veil,
They sight the forceful leader of the wedge
And white-cheeked followers who trail
According to their place along the edge.

So fast the squadron passes in its aim,
The counterpointed song fades on the air,
Trailing but the single leaving strain
Like a good-bye to earthbound listening there.

Flowers speak to us if we will hear. — Christina Rossetti

Autumn Flowers

Caroline Southey

Those few pale autumn flowers,
How beautiful they are!
Than all that went before,
Than all the summer store,
How lovelier far!

And why?—They are the last!
The last! The last! The last!
Oh, by that little word
How many thoughts are stirred
That whisper of the past!

Snapdragons in Late Autumn

J. J. McKenna

They do not breathe smoke or fire,
Of course, or roar at the weather
In fright or surprise, these pure
Golden spies huddled in phalanx together,
Their fires reduced to the last low ember.
Yet this last of the garden still in flower
Resists the season, the fashions of the calendar,
To inspire our unreasoned, our unspoken prayers.

Crimson and white snapdragons fill a lingering garden bed. Photo by David Liebman.

Ideals' Family Recipes

Grandmothers of yesteryear knew the value of a well-seasoned skillet, using it to fry bacon in the morning, heat tomatoes at lunch, and whip up gravy in the evening. Let your skillet try a taste of these family favorites. We would love to try your favorite recipe too. Send a typed copy to Ideals Publications, 535 Metroplex Drive, Suite 250, Nashville, TN 37211. We pay $10 for each recipe published.

Turkey Fritters

Mary C. Stormer of Peru, Illinois

2 cups all-purpose flour
2 teaspoons baking powder
1 teaspoon salt
2 large eggs, lightly beaten
1 cup milk

1 pound ground turkey, cooked
¼ cup finely chopped onion
¼ cup finely chopped green pepper
¼ cup minced fresh parsley
  Vegetable oil

In a medium bowl, sift together flour, baking powder, and salt. Set aside. In a large bowl, combine eggs with milk. Gradually add dry ingredients and mix well. Fold in cooked turkey, onion, green pepper, and parsley. Mix well.

In a large skillet, heat approximately 1 inch of oil over medium-high heat. Drop batter by tablespoons into hot oil. Fry until golden brown on both sides. Transfer onto plate lined with paper towels to drain. Makes 2 dozen fritters.

Fried Chicken with Presto Sauce

Emma Campbell of New Glasgow, Nova Scotia, Canada

1 2-pound fryer chicken, cut into pieces
½ cup all-purpose flour seasoned with salt and pepper
¼ cup vegetable shortening

1 10-ounce can condensed cream of mushroom soup
½ cup water

Dust pieces of chicken with flour and set aside. In large skillet, heat shortening over high heat. Place chicken into hot skillet. Brown on all sides. Lower temperature; cover and cook approximately 40 minutes or until chicken is cooked through and tender. Check smaller pieces earlier. Uncover; cook an additional 5 minutes to recrisp chicken. Transfer to plate lined with paper towels to drain. Pour off all but 2 tablespoons of drippings from skillet. Add soup and water. Heat, stirring often. Serve sauce with chicken. Makes 4 servings.

Root Vegetables with Herbs
Lynda Sprague of Kansas City, Missouri

2 pounds mixed root vegetables —
   potatoes, carrots, turnips, parsnips,
   beets, sweet potatoes, small onions,
   whole shallots

1 head garlic, separated into cloves
   Fresh rosemary and thyme, chopped
3 tablespoons olive oil
   Salt and pepper to taste

Preheat oven to 425° F. Peel all vegetables and chop all into roughly the same size. Place all in a large bowl; toss with herbs and oil; salt and pepper to taste. Place into a large, oven-safe skillet that will hold the vegetables in one layer. Bake 1 hour, turning vegetables several times until they are browned and tender. Squeeze garlic; discard membrane. Turn out into a serving bowl and serve warm. Makes 8 servings.

Zucchini Fritters
Peggy Hill of Goff, Kansas

1 cup all-purpose flour
2 teaspoons granulated sugar
1½ teaspoons baking powder
1 teaspoon salt
2 eggs, separated

⅓ cup milk
1 tablespoon butter, melted
1 cup finely grated zucchini
   Vegetable oil
   Powdered sugar

In a medium bowl, sift together flour, sugar, baking powder, and salt. Set aside. In a large bowl, beat egg yolks; stir in milk and butter. Slowly add dry ingredients; mix well. Stir in zucchini and egg whites; mix well. In a large skillet, heat approximately 1 inch of oil over medium-high heat. Drop batter by tablespoons into hot oil. Fry 1½ minutes on each side. Transfer to plate lined with paper towels to drain. Shake fritters in a bag of powdered sugar. Serve hot. Makes 2 dozen fritters.

Skillet Fiesta
Violeta B. Hayes of Wynne, Arkansas

1 16-ounce package cooked Kielbasa sausage
1 tablespoon vegetable oil
1 red bell pepper, chopped
1 green pepper, chopped
¼ cup chopped onion
1 clove garlic, chopped
1 tablespoon ground ginger

1 1¼-ounce package taco seasoning
¾ cup hot water
2 tablespoons granulated sugar
1 15½-ounce can red kidney beans, drained
1 15½-ounce can black beans, drained
1 2¼-ounce can sliced black olives, drained
2 cups pasta spirals, cooked

Slice sausage into 1-inch pieces; set aside. In a large skillet, sauté oil, peppers, onion, garlic, and ginger over medium heat. Add taco seasoning and water; stir. Stir in sugar to reduce acidity. Add sausage, beans, and olives and stir. Simmer 5 minutes or until sausage is heated through. Stir in pasta and simmer an additional 3 minutes. Makes 4 servings.

A SLICE OF LIFE

Douglas Malloch

Art by Eve DeGrie

POTS AND PANS

Not all the melody life can hold
Must all be played on a harp of gold.
I am glad that my ear has caught the tunes
In things like dishes and forks and spoons.
There's lots of music, I often think,
In the clatter of pans in a kitchen sink,
And every morning a broom goes swish
With all the melody heart could wish.

Why, the finest music that ever I heard
Was not the call of a crimson bird
But a peddler passed with a creaking van;
And I almost went with that roving man.

For his swaying pans and his swinging pails
Rolled and rattled and ran the scales
And filled my soul with their gypsy song
Till I nearly followed that van along.

The gypsy van dropped over the hill,
But it left its music behind it still.
I wipe the silver, I rattle the pans,
And I make a tune like the gypsy man's.
It's really remarkable what is in
A pot, a kettle, a plate of tin,
For the hand that works with a heart that sings
Finds many a tune in the commonest things!

The Open Road Leads Home

Will Evans

If you've come down with wanderlust
And heard the siren call,
Then follow open roads you must
Until you've seen them all.
And you'll behold rare wonders, friend:
The snow-capped mountain height;
Green, sunny valleys without end;
Great forest cool as night;
Vast, timeless canyons plunging deep
With multi-colored walls
That brace a river in their keep
To guide its sweeps and falls;
And far below, the open plain
That runs to meet the sky—
All green and gold with grass and grain,
Pure feasting for the eye.
But there will come a time, a day,
When done's that urge to roam;
Then will you seek the shortest way,
The straightest road to home.

Home is the resort of love, of joy,
of peace and plenty where,
supporting and supported,
polished friends and dear
relations mingle into bliss.

—JAMES THOMSON

Built in 1790, this home in Claremont, New Hampshire, has welcomed many a homebound traveler. Photo by Superstock.

Devotions FROM THE Heart

Pamela Kennedy

The earth is the LORD's, and the fulness thereof; the world, and they that dwell therein. Psalm 24:1

WHAT'S YOURS AND MINE?

I teach high-school students and spend much time at school dealing with adolescent tribulations. But for about forty-five minutes each Thursday, I sit with kindergartners as they eat their lunches, and I supervise their recess time. It has been an enlightening interlude from the intricacies of high-school life. High-school girls are masters of innuendo and subtlety. In kindergarten, the issues are much more plain.

Sara doesn't like the way Amy is looking at her across the lunch table so she says, "Why are you looking stink-eye at me?" Diana thinks my hair leaves something to be desired and remarks, "Teacher, why do you make your hair all frizzy like that?" When I glance down at tiny Chloe, who seems intent upon burrowing her face into my side, she grins up at me and croons, "You smell good like watermelons!" I never have to wonder where I stand with these little girls. Their world is clear-cut and fairly simple; and when we move out to the playground during recess, their somewhat narrow view of life becomes even more evident.

When you're in kindergarten, the world is plainly divided into two camps: what's yours and what's mine. Of course most of the time, there isn't consensus about this, and that's why we teachers supervise recess. We walk around the tetherball poles dodging errant balls and adjudicating disputes. "I had the hula hoop first and she took it and it's mine." "No, you said I could use it and so it's mine." "Your ball rolled into our game, so it's ours." "Is not! Is too!" It doesn't matter if there are four other balls or hula hoops. Only the one being disputed is of interest because "it's mine!" The problem is that the kids spend so much time arguing about what belongs to whom that they often have very little time left to enjoy their recess.

It's easy to laugh at these five-year-olds and their playground arguments, but I began thinking one day about how, as adults, we often engage in the same thought patterns. We become preoccupied about who had it first, whose stuff is in whose space, what's mine and what's yours. In the process, we waste precious time being upset and often damage relationships. We, like those children, end up dissatisfied and grumpy.

Wouldn't we be better off if we adopted the attitude David expressed in the twenty-fourth Psalm? Here was a king who had land, wealth, fame, military success, and the praises of his people, yet he recognized that none of it was truly his. David acknowledged that everything and everyone belonged to the Lord; and once he had done this, it is reasonable to assume that the response flowing from his heart was thanksgiving. When we see our wealth, our homes, even our families and friends as on loan to us from our benevolent Father, it becomes difficult to be too possessive. Instead, we are driven by grateful hearts to give thanks to God for His unending generosity and grace. And in that attitude, we can then extend generosity and grace to others, thus repeating the cycle of giving and gratitude. Once we give up the notion that ownership is ours, it becomes much easier to hold our possessions with open hands. In our thankfulness, we find the desire to give rather than get, to help instead of hoard.

This Thanksgiving let us determine to shift our focus from what's mine and what's yours to what's God's. And in doing so, let us approach each day with grateful hearts.

> Dear Father, I appreciate Your ownership of all things and Your love that allows me to share in Your abundance. Help me to reflect my gratitude through acts of generosity this Thanksgiving.

Two children enjoy an afternoon of sharing. Photo by Daniel Dempster.

An Autumn Day of Rest

Pollyanna Sedziol

I love a Sunday morning still
When autumn mist is on the hill
And maple, oak, and apple tree
Praise God in regal finery.

I like to wander by the pond
Where fern and wild rose drop their frond,
To watch the drake who preens a feather
And plans the flight toward warmer weather.

I like to watch each morning's dawn,
A little sad that summer's gone
And glad of sadness that's made sweet
By one more season of life complete.

And when the evening sun has set
And afterglow still lingers yet,
I too will sing with grateful praise
For beauty blessing autumn's days.

I Love an Autumn Twilight

Grace V. Watkins

I love an autumn twilight and the star
That glimmers silverly above the west,
The crystal song of thrushes and the far,
Deep silence after birds have gone to rest.

I love a candle and the golden flame,
The flower fragrance in the dusk-blue air;
And in the darkness, whispering God's name,
I love the wonder of a quiet prayer.

*A bent-willow chair offers a view of a misty sunrise in Missouri.
Photo by Gay Bumgarner.*

All This and More

Olive Dunkelberger

The freshness of the morning,
The glow from sunset's crown,
The stately form of maples,
The cornfields turning brown.

A bin of ample harvest,
A home of trust and love,

A church for spiritual guidance,
His mercy from above.

These are the heav'nly offerings;
These mold the basic plan.
These are moments of blessings
That bring God close to man.

Our Thanksgiving

Marian L. Moore

When the golden leaves of autumn
Lie rejected on the ground
And the heavy hand of winter
Closes in on all around,

When the flowers of the summer
Have all vanished with the frost
And the harvest of the season
Has been gathered against loss,

As the geese wing slowly southward
Where the warmer regions lie

And the year is swiftly ebbing
With the moments as they fly,

Then the autumn brings Thanksgiving
To our God for all His love.
For His care and many blessings
We shall lift our eyes above.

As the hymns of praise and thank You
Fall upon each listening ear,
Let us offer true thanksgiving
To our God throughout the year!

Mums and pumpkins add color to a harvest festival in Stowe, Vermont. Photo by Londie G. Padelsky.

We Thank Thee

Stella Craft Tremble

We thank Thee for the love of good that lies within the breast,
For the loving power that led us to a country richly blest;
We thank Thee for the Pilgrims, for the little faithful band
Who bravely paved the way for us in a friendless foreign land.

We thank Thee for the golden wheat, the barley, corn, and rye,
For rich harvests in the granaries, for love, food, and supply.
We thank Thee for our freedom, for all blessings heaven sent,
For a beauteous, bounteous nation filled with fruitage and content.

For the Bible that we all revere, our most beloved tome,
For laws that give us liberty, for affection in the home,
For all these things and many more, God grant that no one may
Forget to thank Him for His care on this Thanksgiving Day.

*A grove of aspen weaves a golden skirt at the base of Colorado's
San Juan Mountains. Photo by Terry Donnelly.*

The Twenty-Fourth Psalm

Margaret Rorke

"The earth is the Lord's
And the fullness thereof,"
Sang the psalmist in worship of old;
And the Pilgrims used this
As their paean of love
On Thanksgiving, so we
Have been told.

They were thankful for life.
They were thankful for food.
They were thankful for finding this sod.
Here their people could be
Where the worship was free;
For all this they were thankful to God.

On this day when we pause,
When we gather to feast,
When we're counting our labor's rewards,
It is well we recall
What's oft lost with the least:
That the earth and its gifts are the Lord's.

Gratitude to God makes even a temporal

blessing a taste of heaven.

—WILLIAM ROMAINE

A little church nestles in a valley in South Woodbury, Vermont. Photo by Superstock.

Thanksgiving Table Prayer

Kay Hoffman

We thank You, Lord, for harvest gifts
Bestowed upon us here;
We're thankful too for blessings sent
Each day throughout the year.

We're thankful for the Pilgrims
Who braved the perilous sea
That all may worship here today
In this land of the free.

For shelter warm and family ties,
For loved ones far and near;

We're thankful for each little child,
So special and so dear.

For daily bread in ample share
We lift our thanks to Thee;
Oh, may we share with those in need
Wherever they may be.

We're thankful for this food prepared,
Each loved one gathered here.
We're thankful for Your presence Lord;
You seem so very near.

A farm table captures the autumn sunshine. Photo by Jessie Walker.

Autumn

Nancy Allan

How pale the heart that fails to feel
The depth of autumn's bold, last hurrah
Before the winter snows.
Decked in finery far surpassing
Summer's pastel purity, trees,
Like gaudy, aging actresses dressed to the nines,
Soon drop their finery and stand naked and
Shivering in the autumn winds.
A harvest moon rivals the pumpkins
That decorate the landscape.
Eager geese cross-stitch the sky,
Calling goodbyes to the earth below.
And mums as big as fists
Swell in the crisp autumn sunshine.
Great, trumpeting autumn, working its magic
Year in and year out. A majestic portend
Of bitter things to come,
A grand finale worthy of applause.

A wall of chrysanthemums is decked in golden finery. Photo by Darryl Beers.

The Pheasant

Loise Pinkerton Fritz

There's a rainbow o'er the cornfield
As a pheasant takes to wing
From out his woodland refuge
For his daily feasting fling.
What a splash of rainbow color
As he glides beneath the blue
On this bright November morning
When all autumn's in full view.

Kingdom

Ernest Jack Sharpe

A sedgy field, an old rail fence,
A flaming autumn sky,
And, standing there in silhouette,
A pheasant cock I spy.

No king could ever look more grand
If one would search the globe
Than he with all his royal mien
In brilliant feathered robe.

And nowhere, with the world's gold,
A kingdom could you buy
More beautiful than his appears
Neath fading autumn sky.

A pair of pheasants scans a farmyard in Harvest Moon *by artist James A. Meger. Copyright © 2002 by James A. Meger, Edina, Minnesota.*

THROUGH MY WINDOW

Pamela Kennedy

Art by Meredith Johnson

ODD BIRDS NESTING IN THE FAMILY TREE

amilies are funny. In just about every one I know the members consider themselves perfectly normal. To outsiders, on occasion, they may admit a few idiosyncrasies; but of course they insist that these just hint at hidden brilliance or exceptional and unique talents. However, get a family together on a holiday like Thanksgiving, fill them full of warm turkey and gravy, set them in front of a cozy fire or a generous hunk of pumpkin pie, and stand back. Before long the combined memories of generations begin to shake the family tree; and I guarantee that if

your family is like ours, at least a few odd birds will peek out from the uppermost branches.

A few years ago, relaxing around the table after a particularly delightful Thanksgiving dinner, our conversation turned, as it often does, to "remember when." Someone started telling stories about Great-grandpa Lester. He had been a blacksmith in Maple Valley, Washington, and was built like a refrigerator (or an icebox, to be more true to his time). Lester had a hankering for chewing tobacco and considered the dented brass spittoon an open invitation for target practice. Unfortunately, his eyesight wasn't the best, and his accuracy hovered at about seventy-five percent, which accounted for Great-grandma's dark floors as well as her even darker disdain for "that devil weed." You had to watch your step around Great-grandpa for another reason as well. He was a legendary hugger. Once he caught you up in his mammoth arms, he squeezed like he was working the bellows at the forge. Often he'd set us kids back down on the floor dizzy and gasping for air, our vision temporarily reduced to an amazing array of sparkling stars! With his booming voice, almost toothless grin, and absolutely hairless pink head, he always reminded me of one of those lighthouses in an old oil painting—smooth and round on the top, radiating a benevolent beam for miles.

Great-grandpa had a brother Merle, who had abandoned the farm for life in the big city of Sacramento, California. We visited him once when I was about six years old, and I recall it as the only time I ever heard my mother scream. Great-uncle Merle loved driving but had a disdain for other drivers; he wheeled his big Buick around the city streets and highways as if they were his own. He was of the opinion that stoplights were a nuisance invented to control other drivers, speed limits were merely suggestions, and the requirement to signal before turning was an infringement upon his inalienable right to change direction on a whim. We survived our visit; and, surprisingly, Merle lived into his eighties, although he did spend his last decade disabled after stubbornly refusing to step out of the way when another car tried to back into a parking space in front of his beloved Buick.

Our family tree didn't just play host to male birds, however. Granny Annie, a British cook who immigrated in 1905, was a woman not easily impressed by modern inventions or trends. We never convinced her, for instance, that the characters on her favorite radio, and later TV, soap operas couldn't hear her advice as clearly as she heard their conversations. Her "Don't fall for him, Betty, he's no good!" went unheeded when Betty succumbed to the two-timing doctor. And then, when the hapless woman was left at the altar, Grandma scolded, "What did I tell you?"

Granny Annie also had a unique take on science. She kept a candle by her bed, refusing to sleep with an electric lamp on the nightstand. Responding one day to our repeated pleas about fire safety, she sighed with exasperation and said, "Look, if that plug comes out of the socket during the night while I'm sleeping, all that electricity will just run out of those holes in the wall onto the floor. Then, when I get up to use the bathroom, I'll step in it and PHHT!! That will be the end of me—fried to a frazzle!"

When the space race was going full tilt, she remarked one day, that "this fuss about getting to the moon is foolishness. They're just spending all that money for nothing because once they get there it's going to be pretty embarrassing when they find out it's just a big light!"

Although I have shared some of the more interesting birds nesting on my side of the family tree, ours is an equal opportunity family, and I don't want to ignore those perched on my husband's branches. One of my favorites was Grandpa Morris. He was a true conspiracy theorist and loved holiday gatherings because they offered a captive audience for his latest information (usually gathered with great care from special-interest newsletters and tabloid journals). On different occasions, and usually in lowered tones (because you can't tell who's listening), he informed me that fluoride in our drinking water was a foreign plot to turn us into fossils, President Franklin Roosevelt was still alive and living on the East Coast, the PTA was involved in a massive campaign to subvert the youth of our nation, and the NASA moon landing was faked and actually took place in Nevada.

It may sound like our family tree contains quite a bit of hollow wood and harbors several strange birds, but I suspect yours has its own list of interesting characters too. Although we may periodically poke fun at them, these are the relatives who enrich our personal histories and family lore by adding their own unique interpretations to life. It is they who remind us not to take ourselves too seriously. After all, in a few more years our children and grandkids will be sitting around their own Thanksgiving tables, stuffed with pumpkin pie when someone says, "Hey, do you remember when Grandpa and Grandma used to . . ."

Pamela Kennedy is a freelance writer of short stories, articles, essays, and children's books. Wife of a retired naval officer and mother of three children, she has made her home on both U.S. coasts and currently resides in Honolulu, Hawaii.

Thanksgiving Idyll

David G. La France

Bundle the baby in blankets warm
And break out the coats for the rest.
Cold is the morning,
But bright in its dawning;
November's decked out in her best.

Funnel the family into the car
And travel the well-worn way.
Wind may be blowing,
But we are all going
To Grandma's for Thanksgiving Day.

Brother and sister will be there too,
Each with their own little clan.
Beds we will heap
With jackets three deep;
The family's together again.

All of the children will disappear,
Intent on the games to be played.
Brother and I
Will sit by the fire
And watch the Macy parade.

Soon from the kitchen
    there comes a smell
I remember from ages ago:
Sausage and onion
And turkey, all done in
A way only Grandma could know.

Afternoon comes with a marvelous peace,
A grace from the westering sun.
The children are sleeping;
The grown-ups are keeping
A vigil till turkey is done.

We talk about Christmas, we hang up the lights,
We flesh out our gift-giving lists.
We smile and remember
The many Novembers
That we've come together like this.

Finally the hour for the feast has arrived;
The roaster is proudly displayed.
Grandpa and I
Will lift the bird high
And nestle it onto the tray.

With turkey and dressing,
    cranberries and yams,
The Thanksgiving table is set.
And each in his place
Will bow and say grace,
Giving thanks for the blessings we've met.

Thank you, dear Father, for family and love,
For memories and seasons and time;
As long as I'm living
May every Thanksgiving
Bring interludes equally fine.

A family gathers for a feast in Freedom from Want *by artist Norman Rockwell.*
Image copyright © 1943 by Curtis Publishing Co.

THANKSGIVING AT THE PRATER FARM

Michelle Prater Burke

My father grew up near a rural Alabama town called Fayette. Born in the 1930s, he has often told me stories of life in a time and place when even the smallest boy's days revolved around picking cotton and feeding livestock. When I recently asked him what Thanksgivings were like for his family, I had to coax him to uncover specific remembrances. No scenes of turkey dinners or formal family socials crowded his memory. Almost at the end of a harvest season, November found his farming family with little time for festive celebrations and even less money to fund them. But when Dad thought back to those autumn days of his childhood, he remembered there was much for which to give thanks.

Holiday or not, a typical autumn day in 1943 still required the daily chores for my ten-year-old father, the oldest boy of what were then four siblings. Mornings were spent milking the cows and feeding the animals on the one-hundred-acre farm. My father would draw the water from a well about twenty feet behind the house and bring it into the kitchen for my grandmother along with any eggs she requested from the henhouse. The night before, Dad and his father had chopped pine to kindle the woodstove plus enough wood to fill the box for the next morning's fire.

The stove and two fireplaces were the only sources of heat in the farmhouse, whose original twenty-five-foot, square cabin was built during the Civil War. Now a sitting room with fireplace and bed, the cabin had been expanded with the addition of a kitchen, hallway, and two bedrooms, plenty of living space for a family which would grow to welcome six children plus a wealth of relatives.

A look at a modern-day Fayette telephone book would prove just how many of these Prater relatives have called the town home. Dad always had extended family within visiting range, some of which

gathered at his family's farmhouse for Thanksgiving 1943 and a taste of Grandmother's famous biscuits. Preparations for an autumn feast, farm-style, were well underway. Grandmother was busy cooking for four to five adults and eight or nine children, her well-practiced hands turning effortlessly from sifting the flour for her biscuits to plucking a hen she had selected from the chickenyard that morning, all the while caring for four young children. Although the only store-bought items in her pantry were salt, pepper, and a bit of war-rationed sugar, farm food was plentiful that year. Grandmother chose the year's best from the several hundred quarts of canned goods she put up each summer. My father still remembers the winter night in 1939 when his cold family huddled in an earlier farmhouse and listened with horror as every jar of Grandmother's home-canned vegetables burst in the fourteen-below-zero record temperature, each exploding jar sounding like a shotgun firing in the thin, cold air.

But this year the hard-earned jars were safe, and they would be joined by country ham and sausage from the first slaughtered hog of the season. A few days before Thanksgiving, Granddaddy had fetched the cured ham from the smokehouse and put it into the kitchen's homemade sheet-metal sink to soak. Dried butterbeans and peas were also gathered from their sacks in the barn before being shelled and soaked overnight. Dad had gathered potatoes from the root cellar for Grandmother' sweet potato pie, which was now waiting in the warming closet above the stove; and farm-grown peanuts were busy baking in my father's favorite dessert, peanut butter cake.

Such dishes were almost extravagant for wartime, with rations and shortages greatly affecting the dinner fare at city homes. Dad remembers the night the local doctor came to help deliver Dad's baby sister. The doctor was beside himself at the chance to stay for a

Above left: The author's father (left) and cousin stand before the farmhouse on the Prater farm around 1943. Above right: The author's grandmother and grandfather.

breakfast complete with bacon, eggs, biscuits, and ribbon cane syrup—scarce luxuries to most city dwellers. But with memories of the Depression not far from their minds, the country folk who sat round the table in 1943 were just as eager for their tastes, the result of a year of long days and hard labor.

After every dish was sampled and every tummy filled, the family gathered by the fire in the sitting room. That year, much of the conversation drifted to news of the war. Uncle Laddie was serving in the Air Force, and Aunt Lily's four boys were all in the Pacific. Even in this small rural community, the war was real, and Grandmother voiced her fears that Granddaddy would be the next one called to service.

But even talk of war did not create a somber mood on this holiday evening, perhaps due to a new blessing the family could enjoy together—electricity. Just a few months earlier, the Rural Electrification Act had finally reached the farming communities. My father still has the six-inch box that held two unimpressive fifteen-amp fuses, enough to power the house with six light bulbs and one wall plug. So that year the after-dinner entertainment was music, heard on a Motorola console radio that was Granddaddy's

first purchase of anything electric and that my father still owns and cherishes. The children crowded around the fireplace as Grandmother made popcorn balls by heating homemade molasses over the flames and combining it with freshly popped popcorn. As the evening grew late, my father, his siblings, and his cousins would stand as close to the fire as they could before racing back to their unheated beds. The slowest children often ended up sleeping sideways at the foot of the bed, relying on Grandmother's hand-stitched quilts and heated bricks wrapped in old blankets to secure their toes from the night's chills.

As my father described his memories of that 1943 Thanksgiving, I was amazed that in one lifetime he has seen such remarkable change. I also found myself grimacing at the sheer labor it took to provide for a family and run a farm without running water or modern conveniences. Yet my father's face did not show relief that the difficulties of those days were over; instead I noticed a prevalent smile in his voice, a smile that came from remembering a simpler time when a static-filled radio broadcast and a sweet-potato pie were all that were needed to fill a family's heart with gratitude.

FOR THE CHILDREN

Colt Calculation

S. Omar Barker

Up from the meadow
    the brown colt comes,
        Mentally doing
            his evening sums:

Girl plus bucket
    plus squeaking gate
        Equals some oats,
            if I'm not too late!

Colts, like girls,
    are smart and quick
        At certain kinds
            of arithmetic.

Lantern Light of Long Ago

J. Lewis Schanbacher

It was just an old oil lantern
Offered at a farmyard sale,
Now as obsolete and useless
As the kitchen water pail.
But it brought back ancient mem'ries
Of my boyhood on the farm;
How we rose on winter mornings
Wakened by the cock's alarm,
Lit a battered, smoke-dimmed lantern
And the stove with single match,
Took the bucket, filled the kettle,
Lifted slow the frosted latch.

In the barn we climbed the ladder
With the lantern to the mow,
Threw down hay in dusty forkfuls
To feed horses and the cow.
By its light we did the milking,
Thawed the pump, and filled the pail,
Brought skimmed milk to newborn heifers
With lantern hung on nearby nail.
How that calf would bunt the bucket,
Spilling milk all round the place;
Oft the breakfast call would find me
Wiping calf-slop from my face.

Later years when I grew older,
We would gather for a dance
Neath some lanterns hung from rafters
In the barn. As in a trance
I see happy, laughing couples
Singing some old, sweet refrain.
Well do I recall one evening
Driving slowly down the lane
With a lantern on the dashboard
And sweet Ellen by my side,
When I put my arm around her
And asked her to be my bride.

"How much for this oil-fed firefly?"
Loudly cried the auctioneer.
"Gimme four bits! Bid a quarter!
We'll throw in this bucket here."
No one answered. "Who will buy it?"
"I've a dime," I said, "to spare."
"It's just junk," a young friend whispered.
"Sold! To that old feller there."
'Lectric lights now blaze my pathway
Everywhere I wish to go,
But I wouldn't take a million
For lantern light of long ago.

Lanterns of long ago wait for the next nightly trip to the barnyard. Photo by Jessie Walker.

COLLECTOR'S CORNER

ANTIQUE OIL LAMPS AND LANTERNS   *Laurie Hunter*

I began collecting oil lamps after my family visited a working farm that was patterned after an 1850s homestead and ranch. Everything there operated just as it would have more than 150 years ago. Although I was intrigued with the homemade soap, the freshly churned butter, and the hand-whittled clothespins, it all seemed like too much work to me. But the oil lamps, hanging from exposed log beams inside the cabins, charmed me. Their light was so different; they truly glowed. No floodlights or glaring bulbs were to be found here. Everything was simply lit with the velvety twinkle of subdued oil-lamp lighting.

I spotted my first collectible oil lantern at an antique sale a few weeks later. It was a fairly worn, utilitarian-looking, black enameled metal lantern that I fantasized had been used for illuminating camping trips, church revivals, and similar outdoor gatherings. It was marked and dated on the bottom, so I snatched it up for a few dollars and looked it up at home in an antiques pricing guide. I was surprised and pleased to find out it was really an oil-fueled railroad signaling lantern and worth considerably more than I had paid for it. I hung it from a post on the edge of our family dock when I got home, and pushed off in the canoe after dinner by its luminous glow. Its glimmer was so quaint and peaceful, I was hooked. I needed to find more.

Over the next decade, my search turned up more than two dozen varieties of oil lamps (designed for tabletops) and oil lanterns (designed to be hung), most of which I now carefully display on my mantel. My collection includes a rare Vaseline glass (so termed because of its yellow-green color) oil lamp manufactured during the Victorian era; a sporty 1950s brass lamp base with an amber-colored, tulip-shaped glass shade I found in a retro design shop; a pair of all-glass "glow" night lamps from the 1930s that I use to guide overnight guests up the staircase; and even a bicycle oil lantern with a nickel-plated finish that clamps onto a bike with an adjustable plastic bracket and emits eerie green and red colored lights from either side. Some of the more ancient pieces to my collection are kept in an old cardboard box in the hall closet—rusty safety lanterns that join my family on camping trips.

With all the nostalgia surrounding the lamps and lanterns in my collection, I was surprised and delighted when they were forced to earn their keep this past Thanksgiving! It was my first attempt at preparing the holiday meal, and I was admittedly nervous. Just as my guests gathered around the table and began sampling the dishes, we were all startled when every light in the house suddenly went out. Luckily, the food was already cooked, but a power failure had left us to eat dinner in the dark, at least until I remembered my collection.

I grabbed a few antique oil lanterns and hung them from tree branches just outside the dining room window. A trio of oil table lamps lined the buffet, and more of them formed an eclectic runner down the length of the extended table, providing the only illumination for the meal. Just like I had experienced at the 1850s farm, the entire room seemed to glow.

As my guests and I got settled and began eating once again, I was disappointed to discover the turkey was a bit overdone, the potatoes lumpy, and the iced tea too weak for my taste. But no one else seemed to notice or mind. Everyone was having too much fun admiring my collection, and Grandma was telling remembered tales of how important oil lamps and lanterns had been on her childhood farm. When the electricity flickered back on during bites of pumpkin pie, we all seemed a bit disappointed and agreed we would never forget this surprising Thanksgiving, a Thanksgiving lovingly shared by the light of a host of hand-picked oil lamps—the bright spots in so many special days before and since.

BRIGHT IDEAS

Here are a few tips to spark your interest in collecting oil lamps and lanterns.

HISTORY HIGHLIGHTS

• Surprisingly, oil lamps date back thousands of years, the first versions most likely being hollowed-out rocks or animal skulls filled with grasses which were soaked in animal fat and then ignited. The production of modern oil lamps basically followed this same primitive pattern; lamps were made from stone, metal, glass, and other materials, but with increasingly more decorative styles and designs.

• Animal fat as fuel gave way to whale oil, olive oil, kerosene, and others.

• In the late 1850s, kerosene began to replace whale oil as a more affordable alternative. As this petroleum-based fuel became popular, glass makers produced thousands of oil lamps featuring exquisite designs.

• By 1879, Thomas Edison had invented the light bulb, which signaled the end of an era and began a decline in the demand for oil lamps.

• The Amish, who do not use electricity, still use oil lamps and lanterns today.

• In 1964, an aromatic, smokeless oil was introduced, which revived an interest in oil lamps for entertainment use.

A decorative oil lamp lights a reading nook.

GETTING STARTED COLLECTING

• Oil lamps and lanterns are becoming increasingly collectible, and more are turning up at estate sales and antique shows. These oil lamps had typically been used on a daily basis and are in need of restoration. You'll pay more for lamps that are in working order; but lamps in need of service can often be repaired at lamp repair shops.

• Consider the age, condition, and rarity of each lamp before buying.

• Lamp prices range anywhere from one hundred dollars to well over one thousand dollars.

• Although some oil lamps have been wired for electricity, many collectors search for only oil-burning lamps.

OIL LAMP STYLES

• Ancient Greek lamps are made from terra cotta or bronze.

• Pioneer "Betty" lamps are fitted onto chains so they could be raised or lowered.

• Student lamps feature a highly polished reflector behind a twin wick for greater illumination.

• Petticoat lamps are made of tin and burned whale oil.

• Skaters lanterns feature chain attachments that prevented ice skaters from spilling the oil when the lanterns swung around curves.

• Storm lamps feature glass chimneys protected by steel guard wires.

• The invention of the glass chimney enabled the flame to burn brighter and with less smoke.

• Oil lamps with elaborately decorated chimneys and bases were produced in the late 1800s and well into the 1900s until electricity reached all rural areas.

From a Very New Settler to Her Mother

Edna Jaques

My shack is buffeted by wind and rain;
It looks so tiny on this sweep of plain.
We have a four-horse outfit and a plow,
A garden fenced with wire and a cow,
A few old hens (Dad bought them from a Swede);
I hope they'll lay us all the eggs we'll need.

I feel so rich somehow, for every day
We seem a little farther on our way.
We dug a well and got a steady flow
(Water is very precious here, you know).
It's hard as nails, but still we're very glad,
After the months of skimping that we've had.

The neighbors are so nice, they're miles away;
But one of them was over yesterday.
She brought her sewing, and we sat and rocked,
Laughed at old worn-out jokes, and how we talked—
As if the pent-up waters of our speech
Had flooded all the fields within our reach.

And after lonely months, it seemed too good
To have a woman in the neighborhood,
To tell you how she makes her bread and why
The hens won't set (they just refuse to try).
They steal each other's nests and cluck and scratch
And dust themselves right on my garden patch.

But oh, I don't mind anything at all.
We've got a start, and it will soon be fall;
We'll have a bit of hard-earned wheat to sell.
Our next-door neighbor thinks we're doing well.
And yet this shack so comfortless and wee
(With Dad, of course) is somehow home to me.

(P.S. Don't breathe it to a soul whate'er you do,
But next July I'll be a mother too.)

A young pioneer begins the day's chores in FRESH EGGS *by artist Winslow Homer. Image from Christie's Images.*

The Blessings of the Year, November 1922

Laura Ingalls Wilder

Among all the blessings of the year, have you chosen one for which to be especially thankful at this Thanksgiving time, or are you unable to decide which is the greatest?

Sometimes we recognize as a special blessing what heretofore we have taken without a thought as a matter of course, as when we recover from a serious illness; just a breath drawn free from pain is a matter for rejoicing. If we have been crippled and then are whole again, the blessed privilege of walking free and unhindered seems a gift from the gods. We must needs have been hungry to properly appreciate food, and we never love our friends as we should until they have been taken from us.

As the years pass, I am coming more and more to understand that it is the common, everyday blessings of our common everyday lives for which we should be particularly grateful. They are the things that fill our lives with comfort and our hearts with gladness—just the pure air to breathe and the strength to breathe it; just warmth and shelter and home folks; just plain food that gives us strength; the bright sunshine on a cold day; and a cool breeze when the day is warm.

Oh, we have so much to be thankful for that we seldom think of it in that way! I wish we might think more about these things that we are so much inclined to overlook and live more in the spirit of the old Scottish table blessing:

Some hae meat wha canna' eat,
And some can eat that lack it.
But I hae meat and I can eat
And sae the Laird be thankit.
—Robert Burns

The best things are nearest: breath in your nostrils, light in your eyes, flowers at your feet, duties at your hand, the path of God just before you. —ROBERT LOUIS STEVENSON

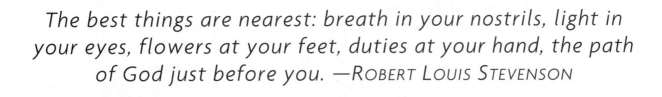

A shaded bench in Missouri provides a gathering spot for a few of the year's blessings. Photo by Gay Bumgarner.

Nancy Skarmeas

LAURA INGALLS WILDER

The facts of Laura Ingalls Wilder's biography read like a catalog of troubles, disasters, and disappointments. Move after move, harsh climates, farming troubles, illnesses, deaths—as the trials unfold it is hard to believe that this is the same life experience that gave birth to the beloved *Little House* stories of the Ingalls family's happy pioneer days. But the stories are indeed one and the same; the *Little House* books grew directly out of Wilder's real life experiences. What the books have, however, that a cold reading of biographical facts lack, is Wilder's voice. In this voice, animated by the lively and indomitable spirit that guided and enlivened the author's entire life, the often harsh biography of Laura Ingalls Wilder does indeed become a wonderful, inspirational, happy story of a family's courage, strength, and perseverance.

Laura Ingalls began her life in 1867 near Pepin, Wisconsin, in the family home that would one day be known to her readers as the *Little House in the Big Woods*. Laura, however, would experience little of life in Pepin. Her parents, Charles and Caroline Ingalls, were drawn to the frontier. When Laura was a baby and her sister Mary still young, the family moved to the prairies of Kansas. There they claimed land under the Homestead Act of 1862, which promised ownership to families that stayed on land in the designated area for five years. Charles built a house and a barn; the family planted crops. Baby Carrie joined the family, and they began to envision a future on the prairie. And then news came that the government had changed its mind. Settlers were to be removed from the area. Not wanting to wait for formal eviction, the Ingalls family packed up, sadly abandoned their new homestead, and returned to Wisconsin to make a new plan.

The Ingallses were discouraged, of course, but undaunted. In 1874 they headed west again, this time to Walnut Grove, Minnesota. The five lived in a dugout in a creek bank until Charles built a house. Once again they began to settle. The girls attended school and made friends. The family joined a church and planted crops. And then disaster struck. A swarm of grasshoppers descended upon the area and devoured the Ingallses' wheat crop. Unwilling to give up, the family planted again the following summer. The grasshoppers returned, however, and the family could not survive the second blow. A son, Charles Frederic, was born in the fall of 1875, and the family remained in Walnut Grove until the spring; but by summer they prepared to move on. Discouraged but not defeated, they moved eastward to a relative's farm to help with harvesting. While they were there, baby Charles Frederic took ill and died.

Somehow, the Ingallses once again found the strength to persevere. They moved to the town of Burr Oak, Iowa, where Charles and Caroline Ingalls tried to make a living working in a friend's hotel. Baby Grace was born in May of 1877. But hotel work did not suit Charles and Caroline, and the family was not content in Burr Oak. In 1877, remembering the friends they had made in Walnut Grove, the Ingalls family returned to that settlement to try again.

Two years after their return to Walnut Grove, trouble came again to the Ingalls. Mary Ingalls, Laura's elder sister, suffered a stroke and lost her eyesight. That same year, Charles accepted a job as a railroad manager in the Dakota Territory, and the family was uprooted once again. After more than a decade of moves and new starts, the family finally settled permanently, becoming one of the first families in the new railroad town of De Smet.

The story of Laura's adult life begins in De Smet. It was there that she earned her teaching certificate at the age of fifteen, and there that she met the young man, Almanzo Wilder, who would become her husband. Laura and Almanzo were married in De Smet in 1885; their daughter Rose was born the following year.

In many ways, the life that followed for Laura and Almanzo and their daughter was not unlike that lived by Charles and Caroline and their young children. Drought and hail ruined crops and left them in near constant debt; diphtheria struck the family and left Almanzo disabled. A second child died in early infancy. The Wilders' house burned down, and they made many new starts in many new places before settling for good in the town of Mansfield in the Missouri Ozarks.

What was different about Wilder's life as an adult, of course, is that she began writing. Wilder took the rich experience of her childhood and began to shape it into stories, which she published in the *Missouri Ruralist* and other magazines. In 1930 she wrote an autobiography called *Pioneer Girl*. Trouble finding a publisher convinced Wilder to divide the book into sections. She enlisted daughter Rose's help and did some rewriting. The result was a book called *Little House in the Big Woods*.

The American reading public proved eager for Wilder's stories. She obliged the interest, and eight more *Little House* volumes followed, tracing the story of the Ingallses and the Wilders from the Wisconsin days to her marriage. The last book in the series, *Farmer Boy*, told the story of Almanzo's childhood. Wilder chronicled her family's life through their many moves. She told of the hard realities of pioneer life but also of the wonderful, simple pleasures of her family's days together. Her books were an immediate success with the American people. Adults read them, children read them, families shared them. Former pioneers as well as people who had never been west of the Mississippi River delighted in Wilder's stories. A television series grew out of the books in the 1970s and reintroduced the *Little House* series to a whole new generation of readers, readers very far removed from pioneers days but nonetheless enchanted and inspired by the Ingalls and the Wilder families.

Laura Ingalls Wilder died in 1957 at the age of ninety. Until her last days she had continued to receive letters of thanks and admiration from readers all over the world. She was fiercely proud of the life she had lived and of the friends and family who had shared that life with her. Wilder was an incurable optimist, never once lamenting that her life had been difficult or full of disappointments and sorrows.

Late in life Wilder wrote a letter about how much the world had changed since her childhood. But she saw some things as constants. Her words describe in perfect simplicity the philosophy that lay behind each and every one of her books: "The real things haven't changed," she wrote. "It is still best to be honest and truthful; to make the most of what we have; to be happy with the simple pleasures and to be cheerful and to have courage when things go wrong." These plain and truthful words embody the spirit of Wilder's writing, certainly, but they are testaments to something far greater—the spirit of the American pioneer. Wilder's philosophy, after all, was not unique or of her own invention. What makes her books so very compelling is not that they are the story of one family, but that they tell the story of countless nameless, faceless pioneer families who lived and died without notice, but whose courage and perseverance opened the American West and shaped our nation.

Nancy Skarmeas is a book editor and mother of two young children, who keep her and her husband quite busy at their home in New Hampshire. Her Greek and Irish ancestry has fostered a lifelong interest in research and history.

SCOTTS BLUFF NATIONAL MONUMENT, NEBRASKA

Christine Landry

My introduction to the Oregon Trail first came while I was in grade school. Once a week in the sixth grade, we played a game called Oregon Trail. The game involved moving a tiny covered wagon across a map of the United States and answering questions about pioneer life. I thought little about how the rugged landscape of the trek must have appeared to the pioneers; I was more concerned with winning the game. But during a recent trip to Scotts Bluff National Monument, a scenic and historic landmark along the Oregon Trail, I was reminded of the game I had so often looked forward to playing as a child. Though the game attempted to teach me about the hardships faced by the pioneers who braved the dangerous Trail, hiking to the top of Scotts Bluff and surveying the surrounding landscape for myself proved a much more meaningful lesson.

Located near the town of Gering in western Nebraska, Scotts Bluff is an eight-hundred-foot, hill-like formation that Native Americans called *Me-a-pa-te,* which means "hill that is hard to go around." The route around and beyond this "hill" eventually came to be known as the Oregon Trail, which stretches two thousand miles in its entirety. Scotts Bluff became the landmark that indicated to the pioneers they had completed one-third of their journey. The Trail was also used by those in the fur industry who took animal pelts from the Northwest and sold them back in the East. In fact, Scotts Bluff was named for a fur company clerk, Hiram Scott, who died near the land formation in 1828, according to legend.

When I viewed Scotts Bluff from a distance, it looked to me like a giant, curving rock of massive size. The Bluff is sometimes described as "a range of high sand hills," which is partly true. This geologic wonder is composed of siltstone, sandstone, and volcanic ash, all of which is topped by cap rock. The cap rock has saved the Bluff from complete erosion. Though the structure is not as tall as it once was due to the winds and water that have worn it away, the Bluff remains a formidable promontory to approach.

Part of the National Park Service, the three-thousand acre Scotts Bluff National Monument encompasses the Bluff itself plus the surrounding prairie land and features numerous hiking trails, a visitor center, and a museum. My first hike at Scotts Bluff was to Mitchell Pass, the place where the Oregon Trail made its way through the Bluff. The early pioneers and fur traders originally followed a route far south of Scotts Bluff in order to continue west; the northern route took them too close to the North Platte River where their wagon wheels stalled in the soft ground. Mitchell Pass, though treacherous, became the favored route after 1850; in fact, remnants of wagon ruts are still visible there today. I was captivated by the sight of the ruts—tangible evidence of those long-ago pioneers who hungered for a better life out west.

My next hike took me to the top of Scotts Bluff itself, although I seriously considered simply driving to the top with the other less-ambitious visitors. During my ascent I watched for prairie dogs and rattlesnakes—two of the area's most prolific species—but saw neither. I was pleased to discover, however, some Rocky Mountain juniper, a scent familiar from perfumes, colognes, and candles. I had never before had the opportunity to view the plant and its blue-gray berries. And once at the summit of Scotts Bluff, I was afforded an expansive and stunning view of the surrounding landscape. Around the bluff, I noted, as the westward-bound pioneers did before me, the first signs of prairie. The landscape

Covered wagons create an image of pioneer days at Scotts Bluff National Monument. Photo by Dick Dietrich/Dietrich Stock Photo.

alternates between brown and green with clumps of grass and yellow wildflowers breaking up the mostly dusty landscape.

Beyond marking that a third of the journey was complete, Scotts Bluff also signified the difficulties the pioneers would soon encounter. Water and food would become more scarce. The mountains must be crossed before snowfall could block their pass. Rat-

tlesnakes and cholera were a pressing concern. As I began my descent down the hiking trail, I was struck by how my trek to the top of Scotts Bluff brought the reality of the Oregon Trail to my awareness in a way that my childhood game never did. Now I will always associate Scotts Bluff with the bravery of the people who traveled the Oregon Trail in hopes of finding a better life at its end.

Domain

Rosa Mary Clausen-Mohr

They little dreamt that time would write their names
With pride and honor in the hall of fame.
Their recompense for weeks of weary toil,
Preparing one small hopeful patch of soil,
Was sprouting seed which greened and grew until
At last the treasured heads began to fill
With gold for daily bread and next year's seed.
Of each small kernel there was urgent need.
In spite of hardships, plague, and drought and flood,
Their work was not in vain; they found life good,
Rejoicing in each growing plot of grain,
And thanking God for seed and soil and rain.
Far wider than the scope of wildest dreams,
Which sometimes glow with strange, prophetic gleam,
Are those vast seas of wheat on prairie plain,
Whose source goes back to pioneer domain.

Pioneering

Author Unknown

We shall not travel by the road we make;
Ere day by day the sound of many feet
Is heard upon the stones that now we break,
We shall be come to where the crossroads meet.

For us, the heat by day, the cold by night,
The inch-slow progress, and the heavy load,
And death at last to close the long, grim fight
With man and beast and stone; for them the road.

For them, the shade of trees that now we plant,
The safe, smooth journey and the final goal,
Yeah, birthright in the land of covenant;
For us, day-labor, travail of the soul.

And yet, the road is ours as never theirs!
Is not one joy on us alone bestowed?
For us the master-joy, O Pioneers—
We shall not travel, but we *make* the road.

*Perhaps this aged wagon once helped clear the road to what is now Utah's
Capitol Reef National Park. Photo by Londie G. Padelsky.*

❖ ❖ ❖

A trio of pine skillets shows the versatility of pine-needle basketry. Image used with permission of Sterling Publishing Co., Inc. from PINE NEEDLE BASKETRY *by Judy Mofield Mallow, copyright © 2001 by Judy Mofield Mallow. Photo by Evan Bracken, a Lark Book.*

PINE-NEEDLE BASKET

Lisa Ragan

America's history includes many basket-making traditions, and some of the most inspired creations include those made from coils of pine needles. Considering the many pine trees that dot the American landscape, baskets made of pine needles began as an ingenious way to recycle nature's resources and create a useful tool. Native Americans have been making pine-needle baskets throughout North America long before Europeans landed on its shores. Both the Seminole tribe of Florida and the Coushatta tribe of Alabama, Louisiana, and Texas celebrate long-standing histories of using pine needles and other natural materials in basket making. The Cherokee also have passed down to their children the tradition of coiling pine needles into baskets and cradleboards.

Another important part of America's tradition of basket making began on the African continent. For many centuries the native peoples of western and cen-

tral Africa have created coiled baskets from various grasses and other materials gleaned from earth's bounty. This African heritage has been particularly cherished among the Gullah culture of coastal South Carolina, where basket making has become an important source of income among contemporary Gullah artisans. The Gullahs were brought to America as slaves centuries ago and have maintained much of their African ancestry, including their own distinct dialect of English and African languages and impressive skill in basket making. Usually composed of sweet grass, Gullah coiled baskets often include pine needles, palmetto leaves, and bulrush as well.

Through the years, pine-needle basket making has maintained a following throughout North America. Today's American artisans who craft coiled pine-needle baskets produce stunning works of art worthy of museums as well as beautiful examples of classic basket styles. Experts recommend that interested crafters seek out a class, a teacher, or a detailed book on how to master the basic technique before beginning their first pine-needle basket. Keeping that advice in mind, some basic information follows.

Making a coiled pine-needle basket begins with a trip out into the fresh air to gather pine needles, also called pine straw. Pine trees that produce the longest needles (ten to eighteen inches) include the longleaf pine (*Pinus palustris*)—also called the southern pine, yellow pine, or Georgia pine—and the slash pine (*Pinus elliottii*). Shorter pine needles can be used but are often thinner as well, which means many more needles per basket and even more patience will be required. Needles may be gathered in spring, summer, or fall, but the best time is early fall when the cooler weather inspires the trees to drop needle clusters. Each cluster of three to five needles actually comprises the pine tree's leaf, held together at one end by the sheath, also called the stem or the cap. Freshly fallen needles are preferred for baskets since the older needles on the ground may become brittle. Each state's department of conservation can provide information regarding what trees might be protected and places where harvesting is prohibited, such as state parks and nature preserves.

Needles must be dried before making a basket because fresh needles shrink as they dry, which would loosen the stitching of the basket. First, wash needles in soapy water and spread on newspapers or screens in a dark or shaded area (for light-green needles) or in a sunny spot (for brown needles). Turn the needles occasionally to ensure even color. Pine needles can be dyed with homemade, plant-based dyes or with synthetic fabric dyes. Light-green needles gathered in the spring absorb dye best.

When ready to begin coiling, soak dried, undyed needles in hot water for thirty minutes. (If using dyed needles, use them while still damp from dyeing.) Remove needles from water and wrap in a towel to keep damp while using. Keep bundled needles straight to prevent bending or warping. Remove the sheaths from each pine needle cluster by scraping them off with a knife or cutting with snips. Experienced basket makers sometimes leave the sheath intact for an interesting texture on the outside of the basket.

Making a coiled, pine-needle basket involves grouping the pine needles, winding them around a center, and sewing to the preceding row. Inserting the needles into a gauge helps to ensure that the coil remains the same diameter, and the gauge holds the needles together as the basket progresses and more pine needles are continually added. Gauges can be something as simple as a one-inch section of a plastic drinking straw or a piece of copper tubing.

The center of a pine-needle basket may range from wrapped or spiral-stitched pine needles to a black walnut or hickory nut slice, leather, pottery, wood, or even a gourd. The shape of the center often determines the shape of the finished basket; hence an elongated oval center will yield an oval basket.

Traditional pine-needle baskets are stitched with raffia—a natural product harvested from the raffia palm of Madagascar. Some crafters recommend using natural, untreated raffia (which can be dyed, if desired), although synthetic versions are available in many colors. Both types are available at craft stores. Pine-needle baskets can also be stitched with strong grasses, palm leaves, or thin strips of bark. Some basket makers use artificial sinew, waxed linen, fishing line, or nylon upholstery thread.

Pine-needle baskets are an example of exposed-core basketry. Some coiled baskets use stitches that completely conceal the core material, but traditional pine-needle basketry uses stitches that allow the needles to show through. Common stitching techniques include a plain stitch, split stitch (also called a "V" stitch), double split stitch, wing stitch, wheat stitch, and zigzag stitch. The baskets can be stitched from the inside or outside, whichever feels most comfortable. Cotton darning needles, chenille needles, or embroidery needles usually work well in stitching the baskets.

Adding other grasses, seeds, pinecones, seashells, feathers, pods, twigs, or beads to baskets creates striking combinations of texture and color. Pine needles can be combined with other materials also, such as sweet grass, iris leaves, cornhusks, cattail leaves, or split catalpa pods. All of these items provide opportunity for even more recycling of nature's resources into beauty, art, and function. Finished baskets can be protected with a coat of shellac or a combination of paraffin and beeswax; either will ensure that the piece maintains its integrity as it is passed down from generation to generation—a true heirloom of a centuries-old American art.

November Dusk

Kathleen Hawkins

The lake's still pink and silvered gray,
Though long since the sun's last ray
Warmed hill and sage and piñon tree
And my old dog and me
At the end of this weary day.

Tip wags when I set the firewood down.
We'll pause awhile and look around,
Close to the sky, windswept and clear,
Breathe in the sharp, hushed air,
Watch lights come on in the valley town.

In black shadowed cedars, out of sight,
An owl calls welcome to the night.
I never heard so soft a sound,
So sad, yet glad. And all around,
The pink and silver light.

But night will come, day is soon gone.
Rested now, we move on,
Holding lake and air and sky,
Holding the owl's soft cry—
Day's last gift. And we move on.

A Labrador retriever heads home after an autumn walk. Photo by Superstock.

Falling Leaves

Henry David Thoreau

How they are mixed up of all species, oak and maple and chestnut and birch! But nature is not cluttered with them; she is a perfect husbandman; she stores them all. Consider what a vast crop is thus annually shed on the earth! This, more than any mere grain or seed, is the great harvest of the year. The trees are now repaying the earth with interest what they have taken from it. They are about to add a leaf's thickness to the depth of the soil. This is the beautiful way in which nature gets her muck. We are all the richer for their decay. I am more interested in this crop than in the corn. It prepares the virgin mold for future cornfields and forests on which the earth fattens. It keeps our homestead in good heart.

For beautiful variety, no crop can be compared with this. Here is not merely the plain yellow of the grains, but nearly all the colors that we know: the early blushing maple, the poison sumac blazing scarlet, the mulberry ash, the rich chrome yellow of the poplars, the brilliant red huckleberry with which the hills' backs are painted.

The frost touches them, and with the slightest breath of returning day or jarring of earth's axis, see in what showers they come floating down! The ground is all parti-colored with them. But they still live in the soil, whose fertility and bulk they increase, and in the forests that spring from it. They stoop to rise, to mount higher in coming years, by subtle chemistry, climbing by the sap in the trees.

The ground beneath a maple near Alpine, Oregon, collects the many colors in its fall closet. Photo by Dennis Frates.

Indian Summer

Edna Jaques

We've got the summer fallow done;
The wheat is in the bin.
And now we're waiting for the snow
To come and shut us in.
To cover up the shivering fields
Beneath its blanket bright
And let the blizzards howl and rage
Across the lonely night.

Above the naked stubble fields,
The brier berries glow;
The stacks of feed are snug and tight,
Like soldiers in a row.
The barns are staunch against the cold;
We've battened up the eaves.
The pigeons in the fragrant loft
Are cooing in the sheaves.

The birds are leaving every day;
We hear them talk and scold
And warn each other to get out
Before it gets too cold.
There's ice upon the water trough,
The grass is dead and dry,
And northern lights are showing up
Against the evening sky.

A bit of Indian summertime
Beneath a golden sun,
A time of lovely gracious rest
From all the work we've done,
A kind of brooding in the air,
An echo faint and thin.
The wind is whispering for the snow
To come and tuck us in.

A barnyard near Bellfountain, Oregon, glows in the Indian summer sun. Photo by Dennis Frates.

November Butterfly

Isla Paschal Richardson

Little bright wings, don't you know
Soon will come the rain and snow?
Can't you see it's long past time
That you sought some southern clime?
Frost has taken all your flowers,
Nectar-filled in summer hours.
Why should you still linger on
With your gay companions gone?
This warm sunshine will deceive you,
Fickle rays planning to leave you.
Do you still seek fields of clover?
Butterfly, the season's over.
Flutter southward, quickly go,
There's still time before the snow,
And I'll think of you next spring
When I hear the robins sing.

An eastern black swallowtail butterfly rests on a bright maple leaf in Missouri. Photo by Gay Bumgarner.

Late Autumn

Enola Chamberlin

Aspens can stand with their yellow leaves thinned;
Maple trees redden and sway in the wind.
Bare boughs reach upward and flail at the sky;
Late-flying geese give their wild honking cry.
But I shall not care for the clouds and the frost,
Nor grieve that the warmth of the summer is lost.
For the nuts are all falling, waiting my will,
And persimmons are ripe on the tree on the hill.

Autumn

Louise McClenathan

With berried branch the year has beckoned fall
And crisped the edges of the clinging leaves.
The old oak hears the wind's clear, rustling call
And shades her acorn treasure from squirrel-thieves.

It's time for popcorn round a glowing fire.
It's time to rake the leaves and pile them high,
To gather chestnuts, and to watch the sky
For geese-clouds, southbound, winging quickly by.

A branch of clinging leaves arches above a river in Oxtongue, Ontario, Canada. Photo by Superstock.

Bits and Pieces

Remember the day's blessings;
forget the day's troubles.
—*Author Unknown*

Gratitude is the sign of noble souls.
—*Aesop*

A grateful thought toward heaven is
of itself a prayer.
—*G. E. Lessing*

Gratitude takes three forms: a feeling in the heart,
an expression in words, and a giving in return.
—*Author Unknown*

Even the hen lifteth her head toward
heaven when swallowing her grain.
—*African Proverb*

A joyful and pleasant thing it is to be thankful.
—*Prayer Book*

The birds have ceased their songs,
All save the blackbird that from yon tall ash, . . .
In adoration of the setting sun,
Chants forth his evening hymn.
—David Macbeth Moir

Gratitude is a fruit of great cultivation.
—Samuel Johnson

I value my garden more for being full of blackbirds than
of cherries and very frankly give them fruit for their songs.
—Joseph Addison

A Day in Autumn
R. S. Thomas

It will not always be like this:
The air windless, a few last
Leaves adding their decoration
To the trees' shoulders, braiding the cuffs
Of the boughs with gold, a bird preening
In the lawn's mirror. Having looked up
From the day's chores, pause a minute,
Let the mind take its photograph
Of the bright scene, something to wear
Against the heart in the long cold.

Echoed Music

May Smith White

I hear late autumn's song though winds are still,
And birds are quietly merging with brown leaves.
Each thing a testimony to a will
As golden fields lie rich with ripened sheaves.

These are rewarding days with autumn's gold,
Bringing faded memories to life once more.
And now we yearn again, like in days of old,
To keep them mirror-bright as of before.

Soft music echoed now will reap its gain
Like bulbs that sleep beneath the snow and rain.

The first signs of winter dust the ground in Bishop, California.
Photo by Londie G. Padelsky.

Readers' Forum

Snapshots from Our Ideals Readers

Top left: Who can resist a baby in a pumpkin? Not Teresa Craven of LaQuinta, California, who sent us this photo of her great-nephew, Connor Craven. Four-month-old Connor's toes got quite messy in his costume!

Top right: Mark and Mary Ann Bateman of Harrisville, Utah, wanted to share this photo of their children, Mason (age six), Mackenzie (age three), and little Mark (age ten). The siblings wasted no time in finding a way to enjoy this pile of leaves in their backyard.

Above: One-year-old Chance Smith is discovering exactly what that large orange ball next to him really is. Chance, the son of Nathan and Mary Lee Smith, loves to visit his grandmother, Ardith Chance, at her farm in Crittenden, Kentucky.